MAN EATING
JOKE BOOK

Run for your life!! It's...

THE MAN-EATING JOKE BOOK

by Claudia Legoff
Illustrated by David Woodward

Hippo Books
Scholastic Publications Limited
London

Scholastic Publications Ltd,
10 Earlham Street, London WC2H 9RX, UK

Scholastic Inc.,
730 Broadway, New York, NY 10003, USA

Scholastic Canada Ltd,
123 Newkirk Road, Richmond Hill,
Ontario L4C 3G5, Canada

Ashton Scholastic Pty Ltd,
P O Box 579, Gosford, New South Wales,
Australia

Ashton Scholastic Ltd,
Private Bag 1, Penrose, Auckland,
New Zealand

First published by Scholastic Publications Ltd, 1991

Text copyright © Martyn Forrester, 1991
Illustrations copyright © David Woodward, 1991

0 590 76580 9

All rights reserved

Printed by Cox & Wyman, Reading, Berks.
Typeset in Plantin by AKM Associates (UK) Ltd,
Southall, London

This book is sold subject to the condition that it shall not, by way of trade or otherwise be lent, resold, hired out, or otherwise circulated without the publisher's prior consent in any form of binding or cover other than that in which it is published and without a similar condition, including this condition, being imposed upon the subsequent purchaser.

Introduction

Hello Human!
Do you know why it's easy for you to tell man-eating jokes to crocodiles? Because they swallow anything!

And do you know where's the best place to get your man-eating jokes from? Why, *The Man-Eating Joke Book*, of course!

But before you start reading, you must chew this over: *The Man-Eating Joke Book* is simply the most bone-crunching, hair-raising, blood-thirsty book you'll ever get your teeth into. With this mouth-watering guide to man-eating beasts you can:

    make your friends laugh ... *their heads off!!!*
        have your parents in stitches!!!
      pull your teacher's leg ... *right off!!!*

From sharks and vampires to tigers and vultures – all the jokes in *The Man-Eating Joke Book* will eat you alive!

If you don't believe me, just read what the newspapers say:

> "Very snappy!" – *Crocodile Chronicle*
> "You'll be gripped!" – *Python News*
> "Fangs a bunch!" – *Daily Dracula*

So be warned, these jokes bite back! in fact, you might be completely devoured. . . . (Yummy, there's nothing I like more than a nice big dollop of eyes cream and a few pickled bunions!)

Slurp, slurp
Best vicious

Your
Man-Eating
Editor

Jaws a few man-eating shark jokes to sink your teeth into!

Knock, knock.
Who's there?
Jaws.
Jaws who?
Jaws truly.

What do you get if you cross an American president with a shark?
Jaws Washington.

What do you get if you cross a pop singer with a shark?
Boy Jaws.

What do you get if you cross a shark with a padlock?
Lock Jaws.

What do you get if you cross a shark with the Loch Ness monster?
Loch Jaws!

What do you get if you cross a shark with a snowman?
Frost-bite.

Knock, knock.
Who's there?
Jaws.
Jaws who?
Jaws one cornetto...

What happened to the shark who ate an octopus?
He was armed to the teeth.

What is a shark's favourite card game?
Snap!

What weighs more – a kilo of shark or a kilo of sardines?
Neither – they both weigh the same.

What advice did the mother shark give to stop her baby being caught?
"Don't fall for any old lines."

"Waiter, waiter, there's no shark in this shark's fin soup."
"So what? There's no horse in horseradish either."

What happened to the yacht that sank in shark-infested waters?
It came back with a skeleton crew.

What menaces the deep and plays the banjo?
Jaws Formby.

What's the best way to catch a shark?
Get someone to throw one at you.

What eats its victims two by two?
Noah's shark.

What's worse than a shark with toothache?
A turtle with claustrophobia.

Why is shark fishing like measles?
It's catching.

Why are some people mad on shark fishing?
It's easy to get hooked.

Which American president do you get if you cross a shark with a hedge?
Jaws Bush.

"What's the difference between a shark and a letter box?"
"I don't know. What's the difference?"
"Remind me never to ask you to post a letter!"

What do you get if you cross a shark with an iceberg?
A cold snap.

What do you get if you cross a shark with a dog?
An animal that barks at submarines.

What shark never swims?
A dead one.

A tasty toothsome of man-eating tiger jokes!

1st boy: My dad faced a fierce tiger in the jungle and didn't turn a hair.
2nd boy: I'm not surprised – your dad's bald!

"Who went into a lion's den and came out alive?"
"*Daniel.*"
"Who went into a tiger's den and came out alive?"
"*I don't know.*"
"The tiger!"

What do you get if you cross a plum with a tiger?
A purple people-eater.

1st hunter: We may as well give up – we haven't hit a single tiger all day.
2nd hunter: Let's miss a couple more and then we'll go home.

How can you get a set of teeth put in for free?
Smack a tiger.

What's the best way to talk to a man-eating tiger?
By long-distance telephone.

"Have you ever seen a man-eating tiger?"
"No, but I once saw a man eating chicken."

"I hear you've just come back from India?"
"That's right – I was the guest of a rajah."
"Did you go hunting?"
"Oh, yes. One day we went into the jungle to shoot tigers."
"Any luck?"
"Yes – we didn't meet any!"

What did Tarzan say when the tiger started chewing his leg?
AAAAAAAAAARRRRRRRRGGGGGGHHH-HHHH!!! (Give Tarzan yell)

Zookeeper: I've just crossed a hyena with a tiger.
Assistant: What did you get?
Zookeeper: I don't know, but when it laughs you'd better join in.

Where do you find tigers?
It depends where you lost them.

Boasting hunter: . . . so I leapt out of my sleeping bag, grabbed my gun, and shot the tiger in my pyjamas.
Son: Gosh, Dad! What was a tiger doing in your pyjamas?

Safari guide: Quick, sir, shoot that leopard on the spot!
Idiot hunter: Be specific, you fool – which spot?

1st girl: If you were surrounded by six lions, six tigers, six leopards and six pumas, how would you get away from them?
2nd girl: I'd wait for the merry-go-round to stop and then I'd get off!

Why is it dangerous to play cards in the jungle?
Because there are so many cheetahs about.

What's the fastest member of the cat family?
An E-type Jaguar.

Did you hear about the tiger who caught measles?
He became so spotty he was sent to a leopard colony.

What's the definition of a panther?
Someone who panths!

Who is safe when a man-eating tiger is on the loose?
Women and children.

A tiger was about to eat a missionary. It had the man cornered, but suddenly fell down on its knees and started to pray.

"It's a miracle!" cried the missionary. "I'm saved! The tiger isn't going to eat me after all!"

Just then, a heavenly voice boomed down.

"You're wrong," it said. "He *is* going to eat you. But first, he's saying his grace."

When is a man-eating tiger most likely to enter your home?
When the door is open.

Who would win a fight between an African lion and an African tiger?
Neither – there are no tigers in Africa.

When should you feed tiger's milk to a baby?
When it's a baby tiger.

Knock, knock.
Who's there?
Jaguar.
Jaguar who?
Jaguar be nimble, jaguar be quick . . .

What did the idiot call his pet tiger?
Spot.

Why shouldn't you pull a tiger by his tail?
It may only be his tail, but it could be your end.

What is a big game hunter?
Someone who loses his way to a first division football match.

Lion to big cat: You're a dreadful cheetah!
Cheetah: You're no better – you're always lion!

Did you hear about the idiot who bought his wife a Jaguar?
It bit her and ran away.

When a poacher put his head into the lion's mouth to see how many teeth it had, what did the lion do?
It closed its mouth to see how many heads the poacher had.

A big game hunter failed to return to his camp one night. One of his fellow poachers said: "He must have disagreed with something that ate him."

Lashings of luscious man-eating lion jokes!

What will a lion eat in a restaurant?
The waiter!

Why is it dangerous to live near King's Cross?
Because it is a main lion station.

Why do lions eat raw meat?
Because they don't know how to cook.

What steps should you take if you see a dangerous man-eating lion?
Very large ones!

1st lion: Every time I eat a missionary, I'm sick.
2nd lion: That's because you can't keep a good man down.

Why is a lion in the desert like Christmas?
Because of his Sandy Claws.

1st lion: Have you tried the new Chinese take-away?
2nd lion: No, when I got there they'd run out of Chinamen.

1st pupil: Lions have a great sense of humour.
2nd pupil: How do you know?
1st pupil: I told some of my jokes to one at the zoo, and it absolutely roared!

Knock, knock.
Who's there?
Lionel.
Lionel who?
Lionel roar if you tread on its tail.

1st hunter: I just saw a lion with spots.
2nd hunter: You mean a leopard.
1st hunter: No, it was a lion with measles.

Did you hear about the lioness who got towed away?
She parked on a yellow lion.

"Who was the man who used to make his living sticking his right arm down a lion's throat?"
"*I forget his real name, but they call him 'Lefty' now...*"

Why were the Colosseum managers in ancient Rome angry with their lions?
Because they were eating up all their prophets (profits).

What do you call a vain lion?
A dandy-lion!

What is the equator?
An imaginary lion running round the earth.

What did the lion say when it saw two hunters in a jeep?
"Hooray – it's Meals on Wheels!"

1st lion: That hunter who camped near the lake last night has been eaten.
2nd lion: How do you know?
1st lion: I have inside information.

Mother lion: What are you doing, son?
Baby lion: I'm chasing a hunter around a tree.
Mother lion: How many times do I have to tell you not to play with your food?

What must a lion tamer know to teach a lion tricks?
More than the lion.

1st boy: Where did you get that beautiful stuffed lion?
2nd boy: In Africa – I went on a big game safari with my Uncle Fred.
1st boy: What's it stuffed with?
2nd boy: My Uncle Fred.

What drink does the king of the jungle like best?
Lyons Quick Brew.

What is the difference between a wet day and a lion with toothache?
One is pouring with rain, the other is roaring with pain.

What is the most important part of a lion?
The mane part.

What do you do when you see a fierce man-eating lion?
Hope he doesn't see you.

A lady was taking her son around the museum when they came across a huge stuffed lion in a glass case.

"Mum," asked the puzzled boy, "how did they shoot the lion without breaking the glass?"

A mouth-watering meal of man-biting mosquito jokes!

Knock, knock.
Who's there?
Amos.
Amos who?
A mosquito bit me.

Knock, knock.
Who's there?
Anna.
Anna who?
Another mosquito.

What is small and grey, sucks blood and eats cheese?
A mouse-quito.

Why did the mosquito go to the dentist?
To improve his bite.

Why are mosquitoes so annoying?
Because they get under your skin.

What do you get if you cross a mosquito with a knight?
A bite in shining armour.

What did one mosquito say to the other when they came out of the theatre?
"Fancy a bite?"

What has antlers and sucks blood?
A moose-quito.

What do you get if you cross an elephant with some mosquitoes?
I don't know, but if they ever swarm, watch out!

"My little brother is so cold-blooded, when mosquitoes bite him they die of pneumonia."

What is a mosquito's favourite sport?
Skin-diving.

What wears a black cape, flies around at night, and sucks people's blood?
A mosquito wearing a black cape.

What is a mosquito with the itch?
A jitterbug.

What do you call a newborn mosquito?
A baby buggy.

Who is top of the mosquito pop charts?
Sting!

Why could mosquitoes be called religious?
First they sing over you, then they prey on you.

"Waiter, waiter there's a dead mosquito in my soup."
"*Well, sir, you asked for something with a little body in it.*"

Two mosquitoes were having a chat on Robinson Crusoe's back. One said to the other, "I've got to go now, but I'll see you on Friday."

A well-travelled explorer was talking about the huge mosquitoes of the African jungle.
 "Are they vicious?" asked someone in the audience.
 "No," the explorer replied. "They eat out of your hand."

What is the difference between a man bitten by a mosquito and a man looking forward to his holiday?
One is going to itch, the other is itching to go.

What goes dit-da-dit-dit-da-dit-bzzzz and then bites you?
A morse-quito.

"Doctor, doctor, I keep seeing this spinning mosquito."
"Don't worry, it's just a bug that's going around."

A sizzling swarm of man-stinging wasp jokes!

What is a wasp?
An insect that stings for its supper.

Where do wasps come from?
Stingapore.

What is the wasps' favourite TV channel?
The Bee-Bee-C.

What do you do with a sick wasp?
Take it to waspital.

If we get honey from a bee, what do we get from a wasp?
Waspberry jam.

Customer: Waiter, waiter, there's a wasp in my soup.
Waiter: I know, sir – it's the fly's day off.

Spoilt child: Mummy, Mummy, I've just been stung by a wasp.
Mother: Show me which one, darling, and I'll punish it.

"Doctor, doctor, I think I'm a wasp."
"*Sorry, I'm too busy – please buzz off.*"

Where do wasps wait for transport?
At a buzz-stop.

Customer: What's the meaning of this dead wasp in my soup?
Waiter: I don't know, sir. I don't tell fortunes.

"Doctor, doctor, I've been stung by a wasp."
"Shall I put some cream on it?"
"Don't be silly – it'll be miles away by now!"

What goes zzub zzub and stings?
A wasp flying backwards.

What do you get if you cross a wasp and a skunk?
Something that stings and stinks at the same time.

A bulging beakful of man-eating vulture jokes!

Vulture: We vultures are smarter than you chickens.
Chicken: Oh, yeah? And what makes you say that?
Vulture: Ever seen Kentucky Fried Vulture?

Did you hear about the scientist who crossed a vulture with a parrot?
It bit off his arm and said, "Who's a pretty boy then?"

"Doctor, doctor, I feel like a vulture."
"*Just perch there a minute.*"

What do you do with sick vultures?
Have them tweeted.

Why don't vultures fly south in the winter?
Because they can't afford the air fare.

1st man: I once had a pet vulture for five years and it never made a sound.
2nd man: That's unusual. Why was that?
1st man: It was stuffed.

Where do the toughest vultures come from?
Hard-boiled eggs.

What do you call a vulture with no beak?
A headbanger.

Why do vultures fly south in the winter?
Because it's too far to walk.

What has a beak, two legs and flies?
A dead vulture.

What is ugly, man-eating and blue?
A vulture holding its breath.

Why couldn't the vulture talk to the dove?
Because he didn't speak pigeon English.

How do we know vultures are religious?
Because they are birds of prey (pray).

What do a vulture, a pelican and a taxman all have in common?
Big bills!

What circles slowly overhead and is highly dangerous?
A vulture with a machine gun.

A crockful of crunchy man-eating crocodile jokes!

Why are crocodiles easy to fool?
Because they swallow anything.

What's the difference between a crocodile and a sandwich?
A sandwich doesn't bite your legs off.

Why is a camera like a crocodile?
Because they both snap.

"Waiter, bring me a crocodile sandwich, and make it snappy . . ."

If a crocodile makes shoes, what does a banana make?
Slippers!

What do you get if you cross a crocodile with a maths teacher?
Snappy answers.

Woman in shoe shop: Can I have a pair of crocodile shoes, please?
Shop assistant: Certainly, madam. What size does your crocodile take?

1st boy: Would you rather a crocodile ate you, or a tiger?
2nd boy: I'd rather the crocodile ate the tiger!

1st woman: Would you wear crocodile shoes?
2nd woman: No, I never wear secondhand clothes.

A woman tourist was admiring a Red Indian's necklace.

"What are those stones around your neck?" she asked.

"Not stones," the Indian replied. "Alligator teeth."

"Gosh!" said the woman, "I suppose they hold the same meaning for you as pearls do for us."

"Not quite," came the reply. "Anybody can open an oyster . . ."

What's worse than a crocodile with toothache?
A centipede with bunions.

Some man-eating library books to get your teeth into

- LOOKING FOR POLAR BEARS by ANN TARCTIC
- THE ANGRY LION by CLAUDIA ARMOFF
- CHASING TRAPPERS by CHRIS LEE BEAR
- SWEDISH LION CUBS by BJORN FREE
- NORWEGIAN POODLES by LIV INA KENNEL
- SNAKE BREEDING by ANNA CONDA
- TIGER HUNTING by CLAUDE BOTTOM
- UNDER MAN'S SKIN by AMOS QUITO
- SAVAGE GUARD DOGS by AL SAYSHUN
- BEWARE OF VULTURES by NORA BONE
- FIGHTING BULLS by MATT ADORE

A vaultful of man-biting vampire jokes!

What's the best way of stopping infection from vampire bites?
Don't bite any vampires!

Why did Dracula miss lunch?
Because he didn't fancy the stake.

Did you hear about the vampire who ate a sofa and two chairs?
He had a suite tooth.

What's a vampire's worst enemy?
Fang decay.

What did the vampire write on his Christmas cards?
"Best vicious of the season."

What's pink, has a curly tail, and drinks blood?
A hampire.

What is the vampires' favourite slogan?
Please Give Blood Generously.

What sort of society do vampires join?
A blood group.

What frozen food company is run by Dracula?
Fiendus Foods.

Why was Dracula lost on the motorway?
He was looking for the main artery.

What do you get if you cross a vampire with a car?
A monster that attacks vehicles and sucks out all their petrol.

What is a vampire's favourite animal?
The giraffe. (Just think of all that neck!)

What is Dracula's favourite breed of dog?
The bloodhound.

What is red, sweet, and bites people in the neck?
A jampire.

What relation is Dracula to Frankenstein's monster?
They are blood brothers.

What is Dracula's favourite drink?
A Bloody Mary.

What is Dracula's motto?
The morgue the merrier.

Who is a vampire likely to fall in love with?
The girl necks door.

Why is Dracula a good person to take out to dinner?
Because he eats necks to nothing.

What do you call a duck with fangs?
Count Quackula.

What do you call an old and foolish vampire?
A silly old sucker.

Did you hear about the new vampire doll?
You wind it up and it bites Barbie on the neck.

A creamy casserole of man-eating cannibal jokes!

Waiter on ship: Would you like the menu?
Cannibal: No, just bring me the passenger list.

1st cannibal: I don't know what to make of my husband these days.
2nd cannibal: How about a nice casserole?

What does a vegetarian cannibal eat?
Swedes.

1st cannibal: I don't think much of your wife.
2nd cannibal: Never mind, just eat the vegetables then.

What is a cannibal's favourite breakfast?
Baked beings on toast.

What's a cannibal who has eaten his mother's sister?
An aunt-eater.

What do cannibals eat at parties?
Buttered host.

What is a sandwich man?
A cannibal's packed lunch.

Did you hear about the cannibal who went on a self-catering holiday and ate himself?

A cannibal came home to find his wife cutting up a python and a small native.
   "Oh, no!" he groaned. "Not snake and pygmy pie again . . ."

What kind of person is fed up with people?
A cannibal.

What did the king of the cannibals say to the famous missionary?
"Doctor Livingstone, I consume?"

What did the cannibal say when he saw the missionary asleep?
"Ah, breakfast in bed!"

What do cannibals play at parties?
Swallow my leader.

A mother cannibal and her son were watching a big airliner fly across the sky.
 "What's that?" asked the boy.
 "It's a bit like a lobster," said the mother. "You only eat the inside."

Why should you always remain calm when you meet a cannibal?
Well, it's no good getting into a stew, is it?

Why did the cannibal go to the wedding reception?
So that he could toast the bride.

1st cannibal: Am I late for dinner?
2nd cannibal: Yes, everyone's eaten.

Cannibal: How much do you charge for dinner here?
Waiter: £10 a head, sir.
Cannibal: Well, I'll have a couple of legs, too, please!

A slither of salivating man-eating snake jokes!

What is a boa constrictor's favourite food?
Hiss fingers!

What do you do with a green python?
Wait until it ripens.

What is a snake's favourite opera?
Wriggletto.

What did one rude man-eating snake say to the other man-eating snake?
"Hiss off!"

What is a man-eating snake's favourite TV programme?
Monty Python.

Who is a man-eating snake's favourite chat show host?
Michael Asp-el.

Did you hear about the clumsy Egyptian dancer?
She couldn't tell her asp from her elbow.

What is a python's favourite pop group?
Squeeze.

What do you give a sick snake?
Asp-rin.

What is a man-eating python's favourite dance?
Snake, rattle and roll.

What do you get if you cross a man-eating snake with a Lego set?
A boa constructor.

What do you get if you cross a glow-worm with a python?
A twenty-metre striplight.

What happened to the snake with a cold?
She adder viper nose!

What do you get if you cross a snake with a government employee?
A civil serpent.

What do you get if you cross a wild pig with a man-eating snake?
A boar constrictor.

What do you get if you cross a snake with a magic spell?
Adder-cadabra – or Abrada-cobra.

What's long and green and goes "hith"?
A snake with a lisp.

Boy snake: Daddy, are we poisonous?
Father snake: Of course we are – why do you ask?
Boy snake: Because I've just bitten my tongue!

"Quick, doctor, I'm being devoured by a man-eating snake. I've only got a few seconds to live."
"Right, I'll be with you in a minute."

What kind of snake likes pastry?
A pie-thon, of course!

Which snake is good at maths?
The adder!

Tourist: Is it true that man-eating snakes in the jungle will not harm you if you carry a copy of *The Man-eating Joke Book?*
Safari guide: Depends how fast you carry it.

What is a snake's favourite sweet?
Wriggley's chewing gum.

What is a snake's favourite football team?
Slitherpool.

Why can't you play jokes on snakes?
Because you can never pull their legs.

Which hand would you use to grab a man-eating snake?
Your enemy's.

Why did the two boa constrictors get married?
Because they had a crush on each other.

What do you get if you cross an adder with a trumpet?
A snake in the brass.

A guzzle of man-eating grizzlies!

What do you get if you cross a grizzly bear with a harp?
A bear-faced lyre.

"Who's been eating my porridge?" said Baby grizzly bear.
　"Who's been eating my porridge?" said Mummy grizzly bear.
　"Burp!" said Daddy grizzly bear.

Why was Goldilocks from such a small family?
Because she had three bears but everyone else has forebears.

What do you get if you cross a grizzly bear with a footballer?
I don't know, but when it tries to score a goal, no one tries to stop it!

"Who's been eating my porridge?" said Baby grizzly bear.

"Who's been eating my porridge?" said Daddy grizzly bear.

"What's all the fuss about?" said Mummy grizzly bear. "I haven't even made it yet!"

Why do grizzly bears have fur coats?
They'd look silly in anoraks.

1st man: Have you ever hunted bear?
2nd man: No, but I went fishing once in my shorts.

What do you get if you cross a grizzly bear with a kangaroo?
A fur coat with pockets.

What ghost made friends with the three bears?
Ghouldilocks.

What's furry and worn by nudists?
Bear skins.

A mish-mash of man-eating monsters!

How do man-eating monsters like their eggs?
Terror-fried!

How can you tell if a man-eating monster has a glass eye?
When it comes out in conversation.

How do man-eating monsters count to a thousand?
On their warts.

What is a man-eating monster's favourite book?
Ghouliver's Travels.

What man-eating monster makes funny noises in its throat?
A gargoyle.

How do English man-eating monsters go abroad?
By British Scareways.

What do you get if you cross a man-eating monster with a watchdog?
Very nervous postmen!

What do you call a one-eyed man-eating monster who rides a motorbike?
Cycle-ops.

Why did the Cyclops give up teaching?
He only had one pupil.

What do you call a handsome man-eating monster?
A failure.

Who appears on the cover of *Man-eating Monster* magazine?
The cover ghoul!

Who brings man-eating monsters their babies?
Frankenstork.

Why did the man-eating monster give up boxing?
Because he didn't want to spoil his looks.

What happens when the man-eating monsters hold a beauty contest?
Nobody wins.

What do you get if you cross a man-eating monster with a skunk?
A very ugly smell!

What do you get if you cross an owl with a man-eating monster?
A bird that scares people but doesn't give a hoot.

Which man-eating monster was president of France?
Charles de Ghoul.

Where do lady man-eating monsters have their hair done?
At the ugly parlour.

How does a man-eating monster get through life with only one fang?
He has to grin and bare it.

Why do some man-eating monsters have Big Ears?
Because Noddy won't pay the ransom.

How do you keep a man-eating monster in suspense?
I'll tell you tomorrow. . .

Why did the man-eating monster go to the psychiatrist?
Because he thought everybody loved him.

A plateful of man-eating piranha jokes!

Man on safari: I'd love to swim in that river, but there might be crocodiles in it.
Safari guide: No, there aren't any crocodiles.
Man: How do you know?
Safari guide: Because the piranha fish have chased them all away.

Who sits at the bottom of the sea and makes you an offer you can't refuse?
The Codfather.

What's pink, lives on the seabed and is highly dangerous?
Al Caprawn.

Customer: Waiter, why has this lobster only got one claw?
Waiter: I'm sorry, sir – it lost it in a fight.
Customer: Then take it away and bring me the winner.

Who has eight guns and terrorises the ocean?
Billy the Squid.

What do you get if you cross a sabre with a mackerel?
A swordfish.

What fish is a mass murderer?
Jack the Kipper.

What does an electric eel taste like?
Shocking.

A crateful of man-pinching crab jokes!

Teacher: Name two crustaceans.
Pupil: Er, Charing Crustacean and King's Crustacean.

Why did the lobster get a divorce?
Because she discovered she was married to a crab.

What do you call Scottish shellfish?
The Clam McCrab.

Why did the crab blush?
Because the seaweed.

Knock, knock.
Who's there?
Michelle.
Michelle who?
Michelle had a baby crab in it.

"When I was on holiday a crab bit one of my toes."
"Which one?"
"I don't know. Crabs all look the same to me."

What do you get if you cross a crook with a crustacean?
A smash and crab raid.

Why did the ocean roar?
Because he had crabs in his bed.

Why was the crab arrested?
Because he was always pinching things.

A terrifying tankful of man-eating tarantula jokes!

Nasty girl to father: Dad, how many legs do you have to pull off a tarantula before it limps?

Knock, knock.
Who's there?
Webster.
Webster who?
Webster Spin, the tarantula.

What do you call an Irish tarantula?
Paddy Longlegs.

Customer: Waiter, there's a tarantula in my soup.
Waiter: That'll be twenty pence extra, please.

What's black and hairy and goes up and down?
A tarantula in a lift.

What did Mrs Tarantula say when Mr Tarantula broke her new web?
"Darn it!"

What did the tarantula say to the mosquito?
"Stop bugging me."

What are tarantulas' webs good for?
Tarantulas.

Teacher: What did Robert the Bruce do after watching the spider climbing up and down?
Pupil: He invented the yo-yo.

What is a tarantula's favourite television programme?
The Newly-Web Game.

A pack of man-eating wolves and werewolves!

Who shouted "Knickers!" at the big bad wolf?
Little Rude Riding Hood.

Why are wolves like cards?
They come in packs.

Knock, knock.
Who's there?
A Fred.
A Fred who?
Who's a Fred of the big bad wolf?

Teacher: Can you tell me the main use of wolfskin?
Pupil: Yes, it keeps the wolf together.

Why did Mr and Mrs Werewolf call their son "Camera"?
Because he was always snapping.

What's the difference between werewolves and fleas?
A werewolf can have fleas but a flea can't have werewolves.

What's the difference between a wolf and a flea?
One howls on the prairie, the other prowls on the hairy.

Which animal has wooden legs?
The timber wolf.

What do you call a hairy man-eating beast that's lost?
A where-wolf.

What do you call a hairy man-eating beast in a river?
A weir-wolf.

What happens if you cross a werewolf with a sheep?
You have to get a new sheep.

What do you get if you cross a werewolf with a flower?
I don't know, but I don't recommend smelling it.

On which side does a werewolf have the most hair?
On the outside.

"I used to be a werewolf, but I'm all right nowoo-ooooooooooo!"

How do you stop a werewolf from attacking you?
Throw a stick and shout, "Fetch, boy!"

A whack of man-eating whale jokes!

Why did the whale let Jonah go?
He couldn't stomach him.

What do you call a baby whale?
A little squirt.

What do you get if you cross a whale with a nun?
Blubber and sister.

Where do you weigh a whale?
At a whale-weigh station.

How do you get two whales in a Mini?
Go west along the M4, past Bristol, and over the Severn Bridge . . . (two whales = to Wales!)

Teacher: What do we get from whales?
Pupil: From Wales? Coal, Miss.
Teacher: No, no – I mean whales in the sea.
Pupil: Oh, sea-coal, Miss.

What did one Eskimo sing as the other Eskimo was leaving?
"Whale meat again. . ."

What do you get if you cross a whale with a duckling?
Moby Duck.

"It says in this book that Eskimos eat whale meat and blubber."
"Wouldn't you blubber if you had to eat whale meat?"

What do you call a baby whale that's crying?
A little blubber.

What do very hungry whales eat?
Fish and ships.

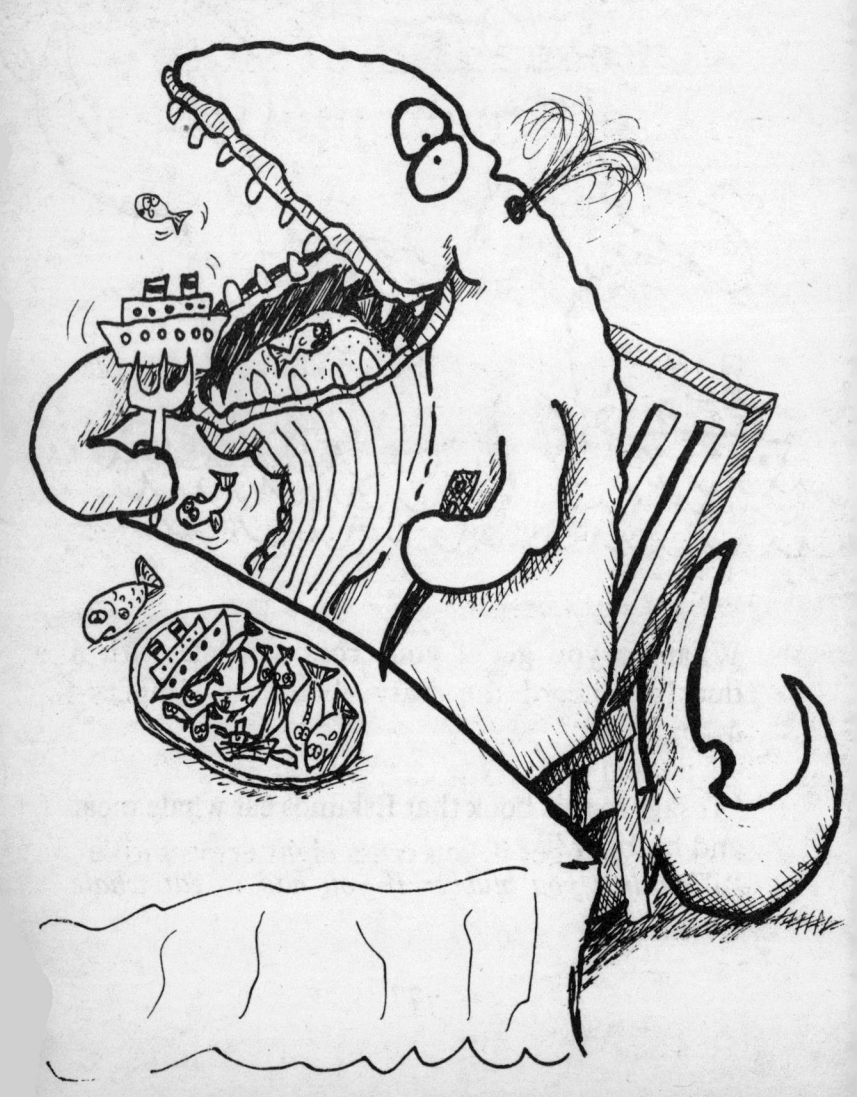

An oceanful of man-gripping octopus jokes!

What's wet and says "How do you do?" sixteen times?
Two octopuses shaking hands.

Why did the farmer cross a turkey with an octopus?
So all the family could have a leg at Christmas.

What did the octopus give his girlfriend for Christmas?
Four pairs of gloves.

Have you heard the story about the slippery octopus?
You wouldn't grasp it.

What do you get if you cross eight arms with a watch?
A clocktopus.

Teacher: What is an octopus?
Pupil: Er, an eight-sided cat?

What do you get if you cross a dragon with an octopus?
An octogon.

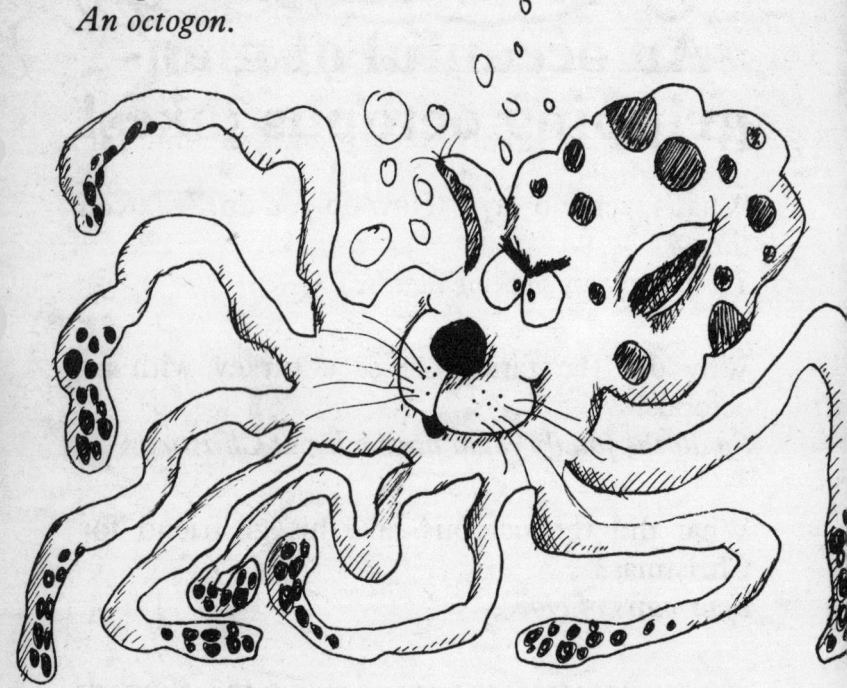

What has eight legs, lives at the bottom of the sea, and says "miaow"?
An octopussy.

How does an octopus go to war?
Well-armed!

Did you hear about the octopus with only five tentacles?
His trousers fit him like a glove.

What do you get if you cross an octopus with a cat?
An animal with eight legs and nine lives.

Who snatched a baby octopus and held him for ransom?
Squidnappers.

What did the boy octopus sing to the girl octopus?
"I wanna hold your hand hand hand hand hand hand hand hand..."

What's wet and slippery and good at maths?
An octoplus.

What do you get if you cross an octopus with a cow?
An animal that milks itself.

What do you get if you cross an octopus with a mink?
A fur coat with too many sleeves.

What lives under the sea and carries 64 people?
An octobus.

A potful of man-eating polar bears!

Why don't polar bears eat penguins?
Because they can't get the wrappers off.

What do you call a polar bear in ear-muffs?
Anything you like – he can't hear you.

What did the polar bear have for lunch?
Ice bergers.

How can you save money on pet food?
Get a polar bear – he lives on ice!

What is big, fierce, white and found in the desert?
A lost polar bear.

What's white, furry and smells of peppermint?
A polo bear.

"Mummy," said the baby polar bear, "am I a completely, totally, one hundred per cent pure polar bear?"

"Of course you are," said his mother. "Why do you ask?"

"Because I'm flipping freezing!"

What do you need to spot a polar bear half a mile away?
Very good ice-sight.

What did the polar bear take with him on holiday?
Just the bear essentials.

Beware of the dangerous man-eating guard dog jokes!

Neighbour: Where's your guard dog?
Guard dog owner: I've had him put down.
Neighbour: Was he mad?
Guard dog owner: He wasn't too pleased about it.

When does a dog go tick, tick, woof, woof?
When it's a watch dog.

Nervous postman: Does your guard dog bite strangers?
Guard dog owner: Only when he doesn't know them.

Neighbour: Come quickly! Your guard dog just bit a man riding a bike!
Guard dog owner: What's the matter with that dog? I told him he couldn't ride his bike today!

Neighbour: Come quickly! Your guard dog just bit a man in his pyjamas!
Guard dog owner: Don't be ridiculous – my guard dog doesn't wear pyjamas!

Scared person: Please! Call your dog off! Call your dog off!
Guard dog owner: Sorry, I can't. I've always called him Sabre and it's too late to change now.

What's got four legs and an arm?
A man-eating guard dog.

What do you get if you cross a man-eating guard dog with a skunk?
Rid of the guard dog.

What do you get if you cross a guard dog with a lion?
Terrified postmen.

1st postman: A guard dog bit me on the leg this morning.
2nd postman: Did you put anything on it?
1st postman: No, he liked it plain.

Guard dog owner: We've just got a new guard dog. Would you like to come over and pet him?
Neighbour: Gosh, I don't know. I heard him barking and growling. Does he bite?
Guard dog owner: That's what I want to find out.

When's the best time to take a guard dog for a walk?
Any time it wants to go!

Teacher: How do you spell Alsatian?
Pupil: A-L-S-A-Y-S-H-U-N.
Teacher: The dictionary spells it A-L-S-A-T-I-A-N.
Pupil: But you asked me how *I* spell it!

Teacher: Well then, how do you spell Doberman pinscher?
Pupil: Don't you know how to spell *anything*?

What do you get if you cross a guard dog with a computer?
A computer with a lot of bytes.

Guard dog owner: You don't have to be afraid of my guard dog. You know the old proverb, "A barking dog never bites."
Neighbour: Yes. I know the proverb. You know the proverb. But does your *guard dog* know the proverb?

Neighbour: We've just sold our champion collie for a thousand pounds.
Alsatian owner: We've just sold our champion Alsatian.
Neighbour: What did you sell it for?
Alsatian owner: For chewing up the postman.

How do you stop a guard dog from charging?
Take away his credit cards.

What's the best way to prevent injuries caused by biting guard dogs?
Don't bite any!

An asteroidful of spaceman-eating aliens!

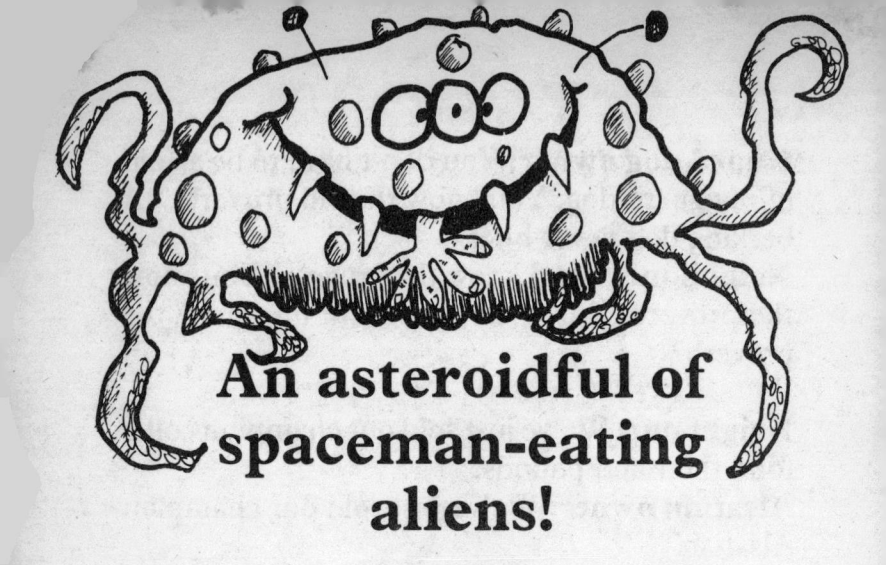

How do spaceman-eating aliens play badminton?
With space shuttles.

What do you call a spaceman-eating alien who's mad about spacemen?
An astronut.

What's horrible and floats in space?
A nasteroid.

When are soldiers like aliens?
When they're Martian along.

What spaceman-eating alien has the best hearing?
The eeriest.

What steps should you take if you have a close encounter with a spaceman-eating alien?
Very large ones – in the opposite direction!

What space film starred a spaceman-eating monster?
The Vampire Strikes Back.

How does a spaceman-eating alien count to 26?
On his fingers.

What's the best thing to say when a spaceman-eating alien points his laser gun at you?
"I give up."

Where does a spaceman-eating alien with a laser gun sleep?
Anywhere he wants to!

Why are spaceman-eating aliens so forgetful?
Because everything goes in one ear and out the others.

Why was the spaceman scared when he met the spaceman-eating alien?
Because of the atmos-fear.

What would you get if Batman and Robin met a gigantic man-eating alien?
The Mashed Crusaders.

What did the space policeman say to the three-headed spaceman-eating alien?
"'Ello, 'ello, 'ello."

"Doctor, doctor, I keep seeing big green spaceman-eating aliens in front of my eyes."
"Have you seen a psychiatrist?"
"No, only big green spaceman-eating aliens."

What did the man say about the ten-legged spaceman-eating alien?
"Don't worry – it's armless."

How does a spaceman-eating alien impress people?
It puts its beast foot forward.

Which spaceman-eating aliens have their eyes closest together?
The smallest spaceman-eating aliens!

What happened to the spaceman-eating alien when he swallowed a bag of uranium?
He got atomic ache.

What's the best thing to do if you meet a blue spaceman-eating alien?
Try to cheer him up.

What do you call a spaceman-eating alien who talks through his nose?
An adenoid.

What's better than presence of mind during a close encounter with a man-eating alien?
Absence of body.

What happened when the man-eating alien was born?
Nothing – the doctor was too afraid to smack it.

Last but not least, the very final man-eater...

What did one maggot say to the other maggot?
"What's a nice girl like you doing in a joint like this?"

What's the maggot army called?
The apple corps.

Who was the worms' prime minister?
Maggot Thatcher.

Why do maggots taste like chewing gum?
Because they're Wrigleys.

What do you get if you cross a million maggots with a famous detective?
Sherlock Bones.

Why are maggots like naughty children?
Because they wriggle out of things.